Trees for Tomorrow

Lynne Patchett

Photographs by Jenny Matthews

Illustrations by Peter Bull Art Studio

A & C Black · London

Contents

Cover photographs
Front – Making a tree record (see page 13)
Back – Schoolchildren carrying trees ready
for planting in Sri Lanka (see page 31)

Title page photograph
Young Corsican pine tree

Acknowledgements
Consultant: David Shirley
Edited by Barbara Taylor
Designed by Michael Leaman
Photographs by Jenny Matthews except for:
p.6, p.19 (bottom) Ed Barber;
p.12 (top) Dr John Innes, (centre and
bottom) Forestry Commission Research Division;
p.19 (top) Morgan, p.26 (bottom) Pearson,
p.27, p.29, p.30 Kloske, Ecoscene.

The author and publisher would like to thank the
following people for their invaluable help and
advice during the preparation of this book:
The staff and pupils of Creswick School;
Forestry Commission Research Division.

A CIP record for this book is available from the
British Library.

ISBN 0–7136–3327–1

© 1990 A & C Black (Publishers) Ltd
35 Bedford Row, London WC1R 4JH

Typeset by August Filmsetting, Haydock, St Helens
Printed in Italy by Amadeus

What do we use trees for?

Look out of the window. Can you see a tree or something that has been made from trees? How many of the things in your home or school come from trees?

We use the wood from trees to make all sorts of things, from models and musical instruments to boats and furniture. We eat fruits and nuts that come from trees. Paper, paint, rubber, cork and even some of our medicines can be made from trees.

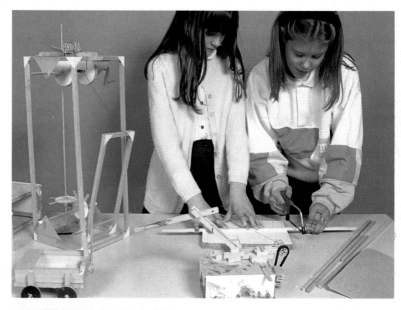

▲ Wood is useful for making models because it is strong and not too heavy. It can be cut into different sized pieces and joined to make all sorts of shapes.

◄ How many different musical instruments can you think of that are made from wood?

Trees around the world

Collect some different objects made from trees. See if you can find out the kind of tree that was used to make each object and in which parts of the world that tree grows. Look up the countries on a globe or in an atlas. You may also be able to discover which part of the tree each object was made from.

Object	Kind of tree	Country of origin	Part of tree
Paper	Norway spruce	NW Europe/Norway	wood
	Corsican pine	Mediterranean	
Table	oak, beech, pine	Great Britain	trunk
Turpentine	pine trees	Various countries	resin
Cork	Cork oak	Portugal	bark
Conker	Horse chestnut	Europe/U.S.A.	seed

You could record your results on a chart like this one. How many other items can you add to the chart?

Some of the most valuable kinds of wood, such as mahogany, teak and iroko, come from tropical rainforests, which grow where the climate is hot and wet. In these forests, new trees are not being planted to take the place of ones that are cut down. And the trees take hundreds of years to grow. It would be better if people did not buy products made from rainforest trees. You can find out more about rainforests on pages 27–30.

Trees for food

Peaches, figs, lemons, cherries, mangoes, chestnuts, brazil nuts – how many more tree fruits and nuts can you think of? Make your list as long as you can. You may need to visit a supermarket or a market to do this. Can you find out where the fruits and nuts came from? Some countries grow more of these foods than other countries. Why do you think this is?

The fruits and nuts of trees contain the seeds of the next generation. When birds and animals eat fruits and nuts, they spit out some of the seeds or pass them out in their droppings. In this way, the seeds are carried away from the parent tree and stand a better chance of finding enough light and space to grow into new trees.

▲ Try growing your own tree seeds. Bury the seeds just under the surface of the soil and keep the soil warm and moist.

How a beech tree develops

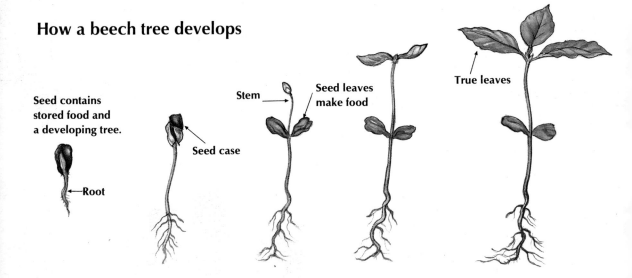

Seed contains stored food and a developing tree.

←Root

Seed case

Stem

Seed leaves make food

True leaves

When a seed starts to grow, it takes in moisture and begins to swell up. The seed case splits open and a tiny root pushes down through the soil. Next, a shoot grows up into the air.

Trees for medicine

For many thousands of years, people have used the chemicals produced by trees, or plants that grow in forests, to make medicines. At one time, as much as 80% of our medicines were based on natural plant products. Nowadays, most medicines are made by chemists in scientific laboratories.

Natural medicines

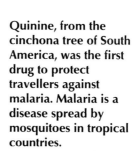

Aspirin came originally from the bark of the White willow.

A rainforest plant called the Madagascar periwinkle has been used to treat some forms of cancer.

Quinine, from the cinchona tree of South America, was the first drug to protect travellers against malaria. Malaria is a disease spread by mosquitoes in tropical countries.

▼ Although modern technology can make many artifical medicines, some people prefer to use natural herbal medicines, such as these in a shop in the Philippines.

What is a tree?

Trees are the largest and tallest land plants. The largest living thing on earth is one of the giant redwood trees in California. Trees grow in many different shapes and sizes but they usually have a single woody stem or trunk. They are also perennial plants, which means they grow on from year to year. A few trees live for thousands of years.

Parts of a tree

1 The crown is the part with the high branches, twigs and leaves. The green leaves use energy from sunlight to make food from water and a gas in the air called carbon dioxide. This is called photosynthesis, which means 'making things with light'. It can happen only in the daytime.

During photosynthesis, a gas called oxygen passes out of the leaves. Oxygen is the gas that all plants and animals breathe to stay alive. If a lot of trees are cut down, there will be less oxygen for us to breathe. There will also be more carbon dioxide in the air because there will be less trees taking in carbon dioxide to make their food.

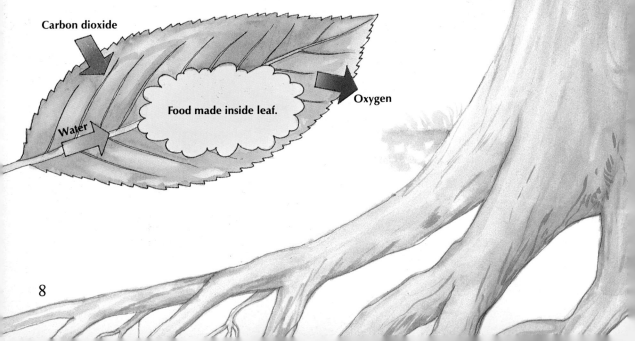

Carbon dioxide

Water

Food made inside leaf.

Oxygen

2 The trunk is the main stem of the tree. It is made up of many layers. The bark is the hard outer 'skin' that protects the trunk from disease, from damage and from drying out. As the trunk grows bigger, the bark grows, stretches and cracks.

Use a crayon to make bark rubbings from different trees. Be careful not to rub too hard or you will tear the paper. What does the bark on each tree feel like? Is it rough or smooth?

Underneath the bark, the trunk is made up ▶ of wood. Wood is one of the toughest materials found in nature. What makes wood so strong? It is made up of hundreds of small tubes, which have thick, stiff walls. These tubes carry food and water around the tree.

3 The roots hold the tree firmly in the soil and help to stop it being blown over. Near the ends of the roots are tiny hairs, which draw in water and minerals from the soil.

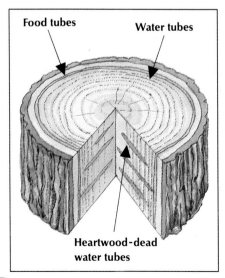

Food tubes

Water tubes

Heartwood-dead water tubes

Trees and water

Have you ever forgotten to water a plant? Without the water they take in through their roots, plants soon droop and wilt. Trees find it hard to grow and survive if the water they take in is dirty and polluted. Trees need a lot of clean water. An oak tree needs about 150 litres of water a day.

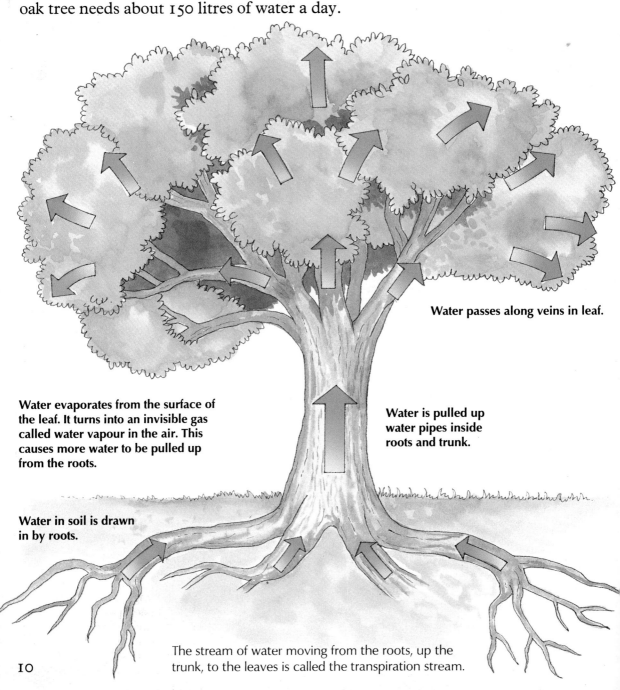

Water passes along veins in leaf.

Water evaporates from the surface of the leaf. It turns into an invisible gas called water vapour in the air. This causes more water to be pulled up from the roots.

Water is pulled up water pipes inside roots and trunk.

Water in soil is drawn in by roots.

The stream of water moving from the roots, up the trunk, to the leaves is called the transpiration stream.

Trees and air

You have to breathe to stay alive and so do trees. Trees and people breathe in a gas called oxygen and breathe out a gas called carbon dioxide. Both these gases are invisible. You breathe through your nose and mouth, but a tree breathes through tiny holes in its leaves and twigs.

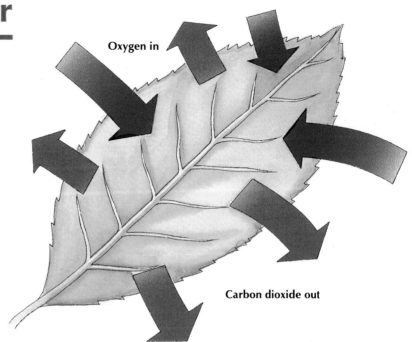

Oxygen in

Carbon dioxide out

Some trees live in places where the air is dirty and polluted. If its breathing holes get blocked up with dirt, a tree finds it hard to breathe. A tree also needs to take in sunlight and gases from the air to make its food. If its leaves get dirty, a tree finds it hard to make food and does not grow well.

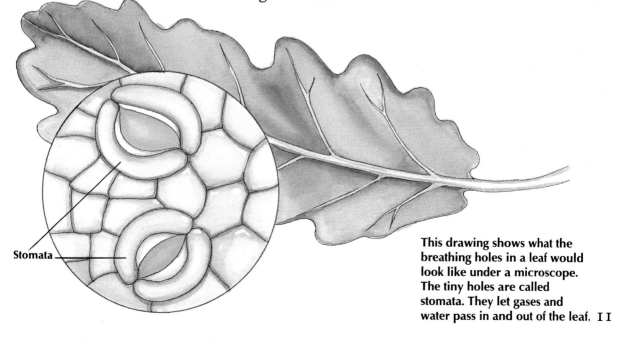

Stomata

This drawing shows what the breathing holes in a leaf would look like under a microscope. The tiny holes are called stomata. They let gases and water pass in and out of the leaf. 11

Acid rain

A lot of the pollution in the air comes from the poisonous gases given off by cars, trucks, factories and power stations. Some of these gases mix with water in the air to make acid rain.

Acid rain affects the growth of trees. It weakens trees by changing the chemistry of the soil around their roots. As a result of acid rain, poisonous metals may be released into the soil.

▲ Acid rain damages tree growth and weakens trees. Trees with needle-like leaves are more likely to be harmed by acid rain.

▲ ▶ In these small greenhouses, scientists are studying the effect of acid rain on the growth of trees. The pipes allow the scientists to control the sort of air that passes over the trees.

A tree record

Keep a record of a tree throughout a year. Measure, photograph and sketch your tree from different angles at regular intervals. Note down any changes. Wipe some of the leaves with a piece of damp cotton wool. How dirty are the leaves? Can you work out where the pollution is coming from?

You could also make a survey of the trees in your area. Draw a map and mark on the trees. Are they on their own or in groups? Can you identify the different trees? Compare trees growing by a roadside with trees in parks or fields. What differences can you find? See if you can find maps of the area as it was 50 years ago. Were there more trees then?

Look carefully at the twigs on your tree. Can you see the circles around the twigs? These are called girdle scars. They mark the spot where the twigs start to grow each year. By measuring the distance between the girdle scars, you can find out how much each twig grew in the last few years. Growth depends on the weather and the amount of pollution.

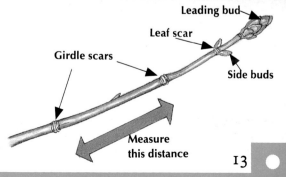

Leading bud

Leaf scar

Girdle scars

Side buds

Measure this distance

The job of a forester

Foresters have to know all about the way that trees grow and how to look after them. They have to plant trees that will grow well in the soil and climate of a particular area.

◀ Plastic tubes are sometimes put over trees such as oaks to keep them warm and stop rabbits eating them. The tubes also help the trees to grow straight trunks. After some years, the plastic in the tubes will rot away so it does not damage the environment.

The trees are grown from seed in protected areas called nurseries. When they are one or two years old, they are strong enough to be planted out in a forest. First the land has to be cleared of other plants. This is done by burning, weeding and spraying with chemicals that kill the plants.

Most planting takes place in winter and early spring when the buds and leaves are not growing. This means the trees are less likely to be damaged. The roots, however, grow more during spring and this helps the trees to 'take root'.

▲ By taking regular measurements, scientists can check how well new types of tree grow in certain soils and weather conditions. This poplar tree is only three years old but it has grown very fast. It would be useful to plant this tree in places where people want trees to grow quickly.

Foresters want to grow trees with long, straight trunks because they can easily be cut up into planks of wood. To make trees grow tall and straight, the foresters plant them close together. They may also choose to plant types of tree that grow fast and have straight trunks, such as Corsican pine or Sitka spruce.

▲ When the trees are big enough to cut down, the forester takes out some of the trees. This is called thinning. It makes the rest of the trees grow larger trunks so they can be sold for a higher price. Large machines are used to strip off the branches, cut up the trees into logs and load them onto lorries.

hese logs come from Norway spruce trees – the nes some people use as Christmas trees. The wood Il be taken to a sawmill and cut into planks or ood chips. A lot of the wood that foresters grow is ed to make paper. Some is used for fencing, for rniture or for building houses.

◄ The young trees inside these tubes are oaks. They are being planted alongside the rows of pine trees in a plantation to encourage wildlife to live in the area.

Plantations

Forests of trees which are planted to produce wood are called plantations. Most of the trees are conifers and keep their leaves all year round. Very little light gets through to the ground so few plants can grow underneath the trees. A dense carpet of leaves builds up on the ground and can make the soil acidic.

There is often less wildlife in plantations than in natural woodlands, but plantations can be developed to encourage wildlife. For instance, fallen trees can sometimes be left instead of being cleared away. Animals and plants can then feed on the rotting wood. Nest boxes can be put up for birds and bats. And as few chemicals as possible can be used to control pests and diseases.

▼ In a plantation, some areas can be set aside for wildlife. People can also use these areas for picnics and recreation.

What you can do

If you visit a woodland or a plantation:
* Don't pick the flowers or damage the trees. Make sketches, bark rubbings or take photographs instead.
* Be careful not to start a fire.
* Don't disturb the birds or animals.
* Take any litter home with you.
* Keep to the paths.

These men are making fencing from the wood cut from coppiced Sweet Chestnut trees.

Using trees again and again

In many countries, some kinds of tree are cut in a special way so that several new shoots grow up from the cut stumps. This is called coppicing. It means that wood can be taken from the same tree over and over again for 50–200 years. Trees such as Sweet chestnut and Hazel are often grown like this. In many coppiced woods, a lot of light gets through the trees so many plants can grow on the woodland floor.

Coppicing trees

1 Tree is cut down to a stump in autumn or winter.

2 Several new shoots grow from the cut stump.

3 After several years, the thin trunks are cut off. More shoots will soon sprout from the trunk.

▲ The stump is cut a little way above the ground. Can you see that the cut slopes away from the middle of the tree? This helps the rainwater to run off the stump so it does not get wet and start to rot. 17

Hardwoods and softwoods

Each kind of tree has a different sort of wood. People who work with wood divide it into two main types – hardwood and softwood. These are quite confusing words because they do not always mean that the wood is hard or soft. The balsa wood that you use to make models is a 'hardwood' but the wood feels very soft! The way to tell the difference is by the shape of the leaves on the trees.

Hardwoods usually have wide, flat leaves and are called broadleaved trees. In cooler parts of the world, most of them lose their leaves during the autumn.

Softwoods usually have needle-like leaves, which stay on the tree all year round. They also have cones and are called conifers. Softwoods usually grow more quickly than hardwoods.

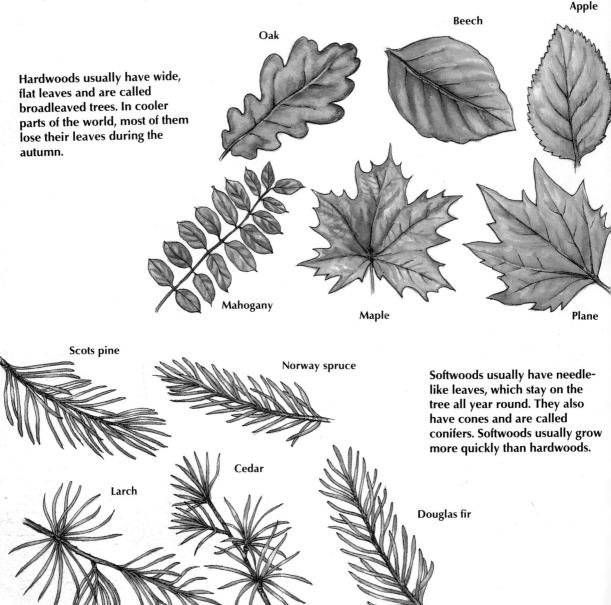

Oak

Beech

Apple

Mahogany

Maple

Plane

Scots pine

Norway spruce

Larch

Cedar

Douglas fir

18

Hardwoods, such as mahogany, walnut and beech, are used for making furniture because their wood has beautiful patterns. Sometimes, a thin slice of hardwood is put on top of a cheaper wood for decoration. The thin slice is called a veneer. Floors, tables and chairs are often made from hardwoods. Almost all the trees growing in rainforests are hardwoods.

Softwoods grow quickly and are easier to replace than hardwoods. They are very strong and are suitable for making paper, boats, furniture, telegraph poles and railway sleepers.

▲ Wood is useful because it can be carved and shaped to make all sorts of things. This sculptor is using wood from lime trees. Lime is a hardwood.

What you can do

* Persuade people to buy products made from softwoods grown in Europe and the U.S.A. instead of hardwoods grown in the rainforests (see p. 30).

* A lot of softwood trees are used to make paper. If there is a recycling centre near you, take your old paper there. For every tonne of paper that is recycled instead of being thrown away, 17 trees can be saved.

Trees for energy

All over the world, people burn wood as a source of energy – for cooking, heating and driving machinery. About one third of the people in the world depend on the energy stored in wood.

When wood is burned, the smoke adds to the pollution in the air. The other problem with using wood for fuel is that trees take such a long time to grow. We use up wood much faster than the trees can grow new wood. And we often don't plant new trees to take the place of the ones we cut down.

What could we use instead of wood? Some countries can use coal, gas or oil instead of wood. But these fuels cause air pollution, such as acid rain. They are also more expensive than wood. The best way to save trees would be for people to try and use less energy wherever they can.

▼In some countries, such as Sudan, many people have to spend a lot of time every day searching for wood to use as fuel.

One way of producing more wood for fuel has been to plant fast-growing trees, such as eucalyptus. In warm countries, eucalyptus takes only ten years to grow into mature trees. Eucalyptus burns well and can also be used to make medicines and paper. Many scientists and farmers, however, believe that eucalyptus trees are a menace. They say they take goodness out of the soil, use up too much water, and release poisons from their roots, which kill other plants.

Eucalyptus trees come from Australia and when they are planted in other countries, they upset the balance of the local wildlife. All living things are linked to each other and to their environment. Before we try and change the natural environment in one way, we should think carefully about other changes that follow as a result of our actions.

Trees for wildlife

Trees provide food, homes and shelter for a rich variety of wildlife. Some of the plants and animals are easy to spot. Birds and mammals feed and nest among the leaves and climbing plants such as ivy and honeysuckle twine around the trunk. Other wildlife is more difficult to find because it is smaller and is often hidden under the leaves or bark. Even one tree is home to thousands or even millions of insects.

See if you can find out about the wildlife that lives in different woodlands, such as oak woods and pine woods.

The plants and animals in a woodland are linked together in a complex web of life. One of the ways that plants and animals are linked together is through the food they eat. These feeding links are called food chains.

▲ Use a magnifying glass to look closely at tree bark. Can you see any insects or other small creatures in the cracks? Don't forget to look out for plants too!

Leaf litter

The dead leaves or 'leaf litter' that piles up at the bottom of trees and hedges provides homes and food for a wide range of animals and plants. Collect some leaf litter and use a stick to separate out the leaves. Do the leaves fall apart easily? Did you find any leaves that have been eaten away so only the skeleton is left? Make a display of the different types of leaves.

Which kinds of small creatures can you spot? You will see more creatures if you leave the leaf litter in a light, warm room for a while. Can you work out why? There will probably be beetles, ants, millipedes and spiders in the litter. How many creatures can you identify? After you have finished looking at the litter, put it back under a tree again.

As living things feed on leaf litter, they break the leaves up into small pieces. Eventually the leaves become part of the soil. The goodness in the leaves makes the soil rich, which helps trees to grow tall and strong. In the natural environment, nothing is wasted.

Protecting the soil

Soil is very precious and forms slowly over many years. Tree roots help to bind the soil together. If trees are cut down, the soil may be blown away by the wind or washed away by the rain. This is called soil erosion.

A lot of trees have been cut down in the Himalayan mountains in northern India. Because there are less trees to 'soak up' water and hold the soil together, more water pours down the mountains. This is one of the reasons for flooding in countries such as Bangladesh, which are at the bottom of the mountains. Cutting down trees in one country can have an important effect on the soils and weather in another country.

▲ The trees on this Ethiopian hillside have been cut down and will no longer protect the soil. Some of the droughts and famines in Africa have been partly caused by tree felling and soil erosion, which make it difficult to grow food crops.

▼ One way to stop soil erosion is to plant new trees, which will protect the soil. These young trees are part of a forestry project in Ethiopia. They will soon be big enough to be planted out in the countryside.

Soil erosion test

1 Find two seed trays that are the same size. If there are no holes in the bottom, ask an adult to help you make some.

2 Put some soil in one tray and a mixture of soil and cress plants in the other tray.

3 Pour the same amount of water on to each tray in turn.

4 How much water and soil comes out of the holes in each tray? How do the plants help to hold soil and water in the tray?

5 Try making ridges in the soil and pour on some more water. Does this make a difference to the results of the test?

To stop soil erosion, people sometimes pile up the soil into banks called terraces. This helps to stop the soil being washed away.

Disappearing forests

For thousands of years, people have cut down forests to use the wood or to make space for villages, crops or grazing animals. Using a metal hand axe, it may take two men a day to chop down a large tree.

Nowadays, we have powerful machines that can 'eat up' forests with frightening speed. Giant forest trees can be felled by machines in a few minutes.

One special type of forest is disappearing faster than you can possibly imagine. Since 1945, over half the world's rainforests have disappeared. And in the time it takes you to read this page, another 81 hectares will have been cut down. That's the same area as 162 soccer pitches. On the next page you can find out why rainforests are being destroyed and why they are so important to life on planet earth.

▲ Without special machines, it takes a person a long time to clear an area of trees.

◄ These trees in a tropical rainforest in the Philippines took hundreds of years to grow but only a few minutes to chop down.

Save the rainforests

Rainforests cover only 6% of the earth's surface but they are home to the greatest variety of wildlife in the world. About half of all the species in the world live in the rainforests. An area of rainforest measuring ten square kilometres can contain 1,500 species of flowering plants – as many as in the whole of Britain. And 400 different kinds of insect can live on one rainforest tree.

Many of the plants we use for food or medicines came from the rainforests.

One in four of the drugs in your chemist contain chemicals developed from rainforests species. Many more life-saving drugs and new food plants are waiting to be discovered – if we don't destroy the rainforests first.

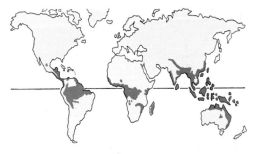

▼ Rainforests, such as this one in Papua New Guinea, are home to a huge variety of different plants.

▲ This map shows where rainforests grow. They are mainly on or near the equator where the climate is hot and wet all year round.

Like all forests, rainforests have an important influence on the weather. The large areas of trees act like a huge sponge, drinking in the rain that soaks into the soil and putting water back into the atmosphere – see page 10. As the trees breathe and make food, they also change the balance of gases in the air – see pages 8 and 11. So although the rainforests may not grow in your part of the world, they may affect your weather.

Rainforests cover large areas and if the trees are cut down, there will be more carbon dioxide in the air. Remember, trees take in carbon dioxide to make their food. Carbon dioxide acts like the glass in a greenhouse. It lets in the sun's heat but stops some of this heat from escaping out into space. With more carbon dioxide in the air, the earth will warm up – this is called the greenhouse effect. Some scientists think this is already happening.

The greenhouse effect

Heat from sun reaches earth

Glass or carbon dioxide stops some of heat escaping

Greenhouse or earth warms up

▲ This rainforest in Papua New Guinea is being cleared so that crops can be grown on the land.

Why are rainforests destroyed? They grow in some of the poorest countries of the world. By selling wood and other rainforest products, people can make a lot of money very quickly. This can help to provide homes, schools and hospitals, which are badly needed.

Much of the rainforest is being cut down and turned into grassland for grazing cattle or growing crops. But rainforest soils are usually very poor and when the trees are cut down, their goodness is soon washed away. So more rainforest has to be cut down to grow more crops or graze more cattle.

▲ In rainforests, such as this one in Malaya, the easiest and cheapest way to transport logs is often to float them down the rivers.

29

Digging for oil and metals in the soil underneath the rainforests means the trees have to be cut down and roads built through the forest. Poisons from the mines can leak into the soil and rivers. The people causing the damage often work for international companies.

Can anything be done? Richer countries could give more aid of all kinds so there would be less need to cut down the rainforests. We could also try to develop ways of farming and using the rainforest that will not destroy it. Some areas of rainforest could be preserved as National Parks.

What you can do

* Persuade your relatives and friends not to buy furniture made from rainforest trees, such as mahogany and teak. Ask in the shops where the wood comes from.

* Don't buy carvings or other crafts made from rainforest plants and animals.

* Write letters, put up posters and go on marches to protest against the destruction of the rainforests.

▲ Dams, such as this one in Australia, are being built in rainforests to use the power of the water in the rivers to provide energy. A large lake forms behind the dam, flooding the forest. It is expensive to cut down the trees first, so they are usually just left to rot under the water. As this happens, the trees make the water acidic. The acid water damages the machinery inside the dam.

Planting new trees

Can you imagine living in a world without trees? Your life would be very different and so would the life of the earth you live on.

Trees take a long time to grow, so if there are going to be enough trees for tomorrow, we must plant more trees today.

What you can do

✻ Join a tree planting group and help to plant new trees in your area. Persuade your friends and relatives to plant trees.

✻ Write to a local environmental group and offer to help them.

✻ Protest against trees being cut down and help to find alternative solutions to problems so that trees do not have to be cut down.

▶ These children are planning where to plant new trees in their school grounds. The white posts mark the places where they would like to plant their trees.

◀ These young trees are ready for planting in the Philippines.

Useful Addresses

If you would like to find out more about the ideas in this book, write to any of these organisations:

Botanical Society of the British Isles, c/o Department of Botany, The Natural History Museum, Cromwell Road, London SW7 5BD.

British Trust for Conservation Volunteers, 36 St Mary's Street, Wallingford, Oxon OX10 OEU.

Common Ground, 45 Shelton Street, London WC2N 9HJ.

Council for Environmental Education, School of Education, University of Reading, London Road, Reading, RG1 5AQ.

Council for the Protection of Rural England, 4 Hobart Place, London SW1Y OHY.

Countryside Commission, 30–32 Southampton Street, London WC2E 7RA.

Forestry Commission, Great Eastern House, Cambridge, CB1 2DU.

Friends of the Earth (UK), 26–28 Underwood Street, London N1 7JQ.

Friends of the Earth (Australia), Chain Reaction Co-operative, P. O. Box 530E, Melbourne, Victoria 3001.

Friends of the Earth (New Zealand), P. O. Box 39–065, Aukland West.

Men of the Trees, Cranley down, Crawley, West Sussex RH10 4HL.

Nature Conservancy Council, Northminster House, Peterborough PE1 1UA.

Tree Council, 35 Belgrave Square, London SW1X 8QN.

Watch, 22 The Green, Nettleham, Lincoln LN2 2NR.

Woodland Trust Autumn Park, Sysan Road, Grantham, Lincolnshire, NG31 6LL.

World-Wide Fund for Nature (WWF), Panda House, Weyside Park, Godalming, Surrey, GU7 1XR.

Index